# There's No Business Like SOUL Business

# DOUG MARLETTE

PEACHTREE PUBLISHERS, LTD.

*For my firstborn, Jackson Douglas Marlette*

# Meet The Preacher...

REVEREND WILL B. DUNN IS JUST A SIMPLE COUNTRY PREACHER...

PEWER'S PROFILE

### REV. WILL B. DUNN

HOME: Bypass, USA.

AGE: Younger than Methusaleh.

OCCUPATION: Expert in Human Relations.

HOBBIES: Spiritual Aerobics, Soaps, Ministry to Domestic Animals.

LATEST ACCOMPLISHMENT: Teakwood deck around Baptismal pool.

GOALS: His own personal satellite and an unlisted "800" number.

QUOTE: "There's no business like soul business!"

DRINK: Pewer's grape juice — Communion, or on the rocks.

...TO A SMALL, BUT DEEPLY TROUBLED CONGREGATION...

... A CONTEMPORARY PASTOR...

... AN EXPERT IN HUMAN RELATIONS...

## ...A SENSITIVE COUNSELOR TO THE YOUNG...

## ... A MAN OF PRAYER...

... CALLED TO MINISTER TO THE FABULOUSLY WELL-TO-DO ...

... HE BRINGS HIS EXTRAORDINARY EMPATHIC GIFTS TO HIS
ADVICE COLUMN IN THE "BYPASS BUGLE"...

...SO FOR THIS HUMBLE HOLY MAN IT WAS A NATURAL STEP FROM PRINT TO BROADCASTING...

...AND THE REST IS SOUL BUSINESS HISTORY!...

# 1 Heeerre's Preacher!

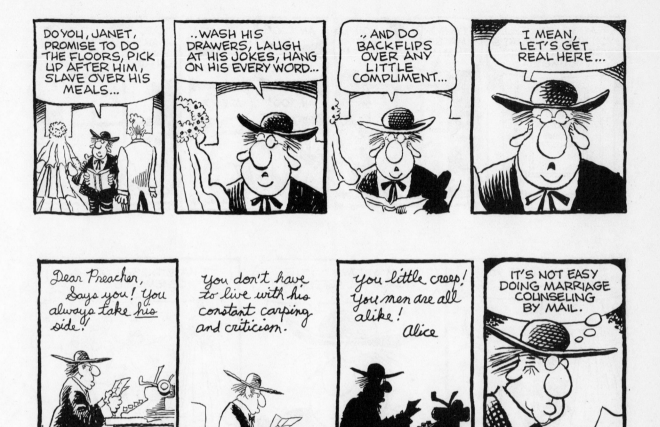

# 3 Human Relations Is My Business

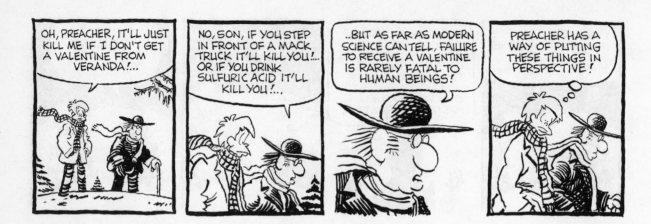

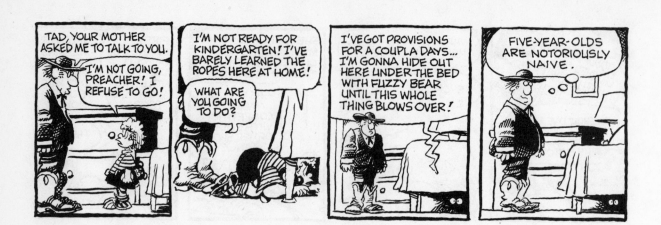

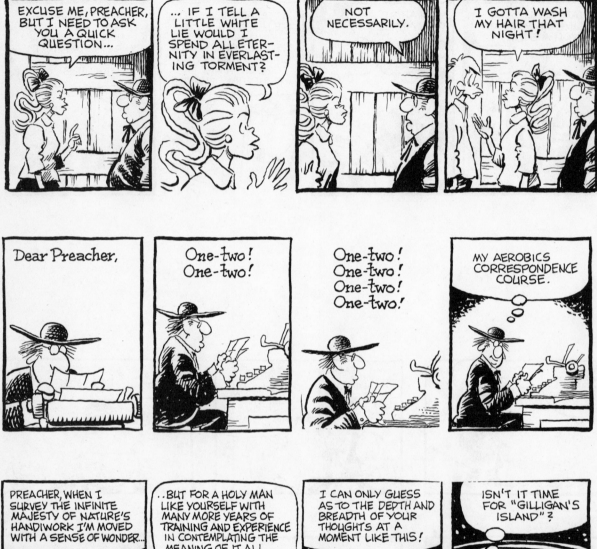

# 4 Happy Trails . . .

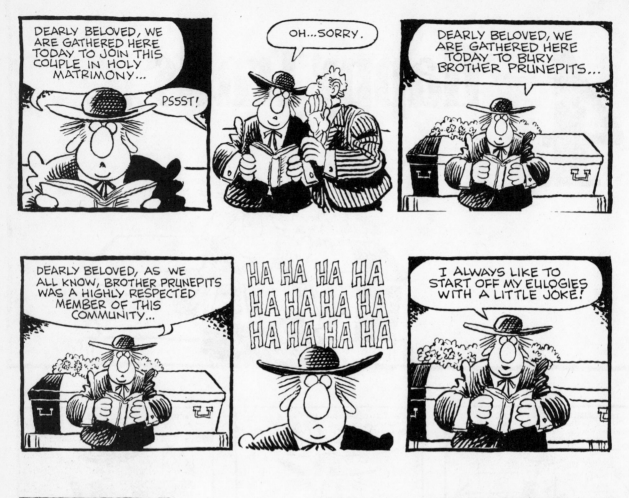

# 5 Take My Congregation... Please!

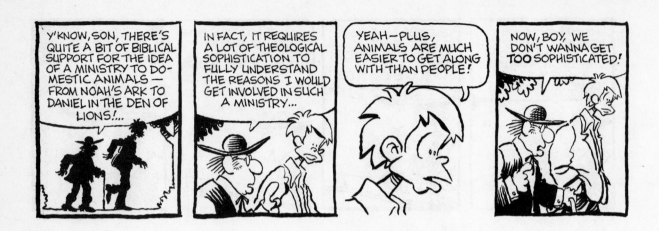

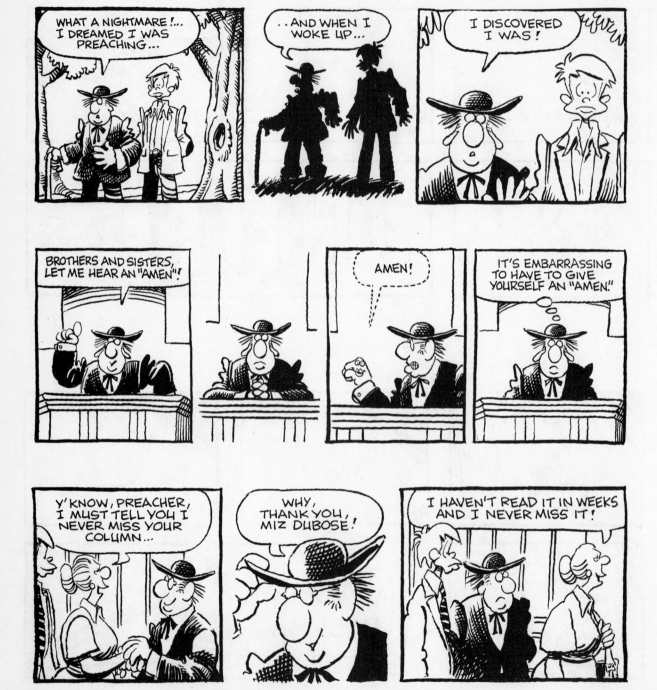

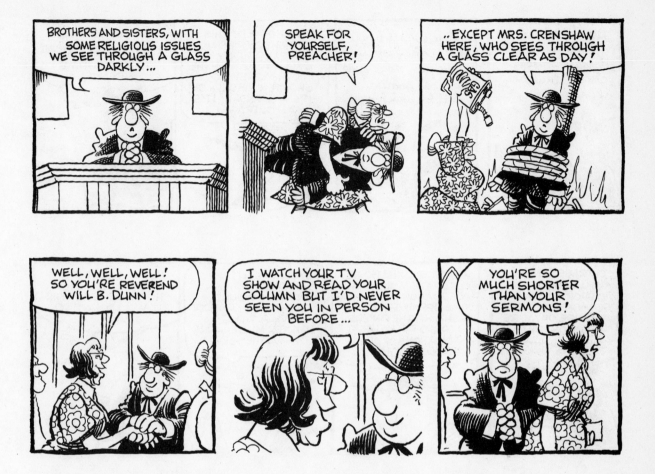

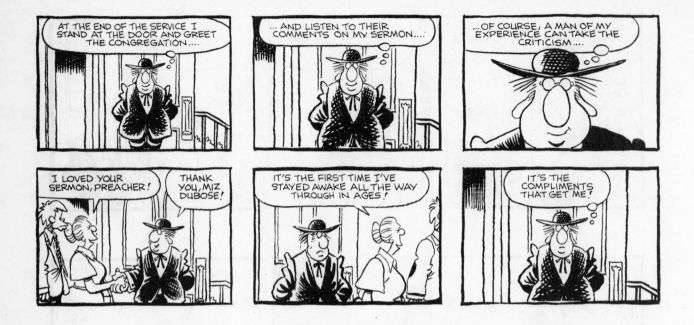

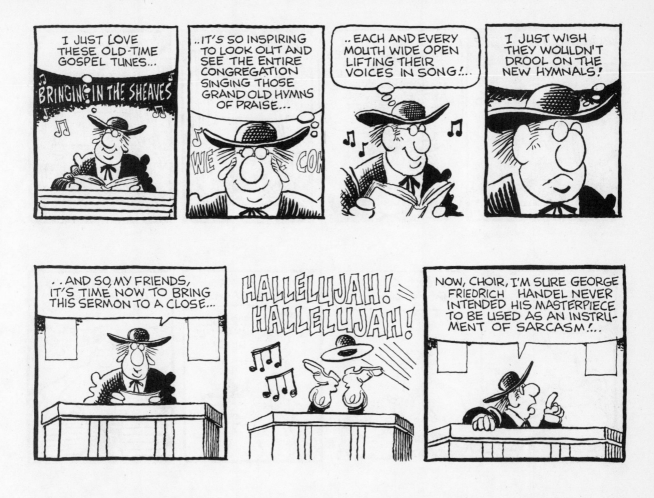

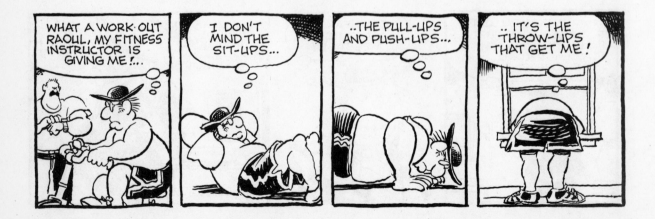

# "Meet My MAKER"

**Doug Marlette** was born into a family of timber wolves, but was kidnapped at an early age by a marauding band of Southern debutantes. Raised among them, he learned their ways.

For years, he eked out a living as an itinerant cartoon laborer, following the chuckles harvests season to season, town to town. Today he draws award-winning editorial cartoons for The Charlotte Observer, and is occasionally spotted howling at the moon.

The only cartoonist awarded a Nieman Fellowship at Harvard University, Marlette spent that year developing his mild regional drawl, an attention-grabber in Cambridge, into a full-fledged affectation.

Returning home to Charlotte he immediately began perpetrating his hilarious autobiographical comic strip, Kudzu.

Asked what sort of theological background was necessary to create the classic comic character, the Rev. Will B. Dunn, the cartoonist explains, "I know all the lyrics to 'Amazing Grace' by heart."